Dangerous DINOSAURS

Gareth Stevens
Publishing

Please visit our Web site www.garethstevens.com. For a free color catalog of all our high-quality books, call toll free 1-800-542-2595 or fax 1-877-542-2596.

Library of Congress Cataloging-in-Publication Data
Jackson, Tom.
Dangerous dinosaurs / Tom Jackson.
   p. cm. – (Dangerous animals)
Includes index.
 ISBN 978-1-4339-4037-8 (lib. bdg.)
 ISBN 978-1-4339-4038-5 (pbk.)
 ISBN 978-1-4339-4039-2 (6-pack)
1. Dinosaurs–Juvenile literature. 2. Dinosaurs–Behavior–Juvenile literature. 3. Predatory animals–Juvenile literature. I. Title.
 QE861.5.J33 2011
 567.9–dc22

                              2010011542

Published in 2011 by
Gareth Stevens Publishing
111 East 14th Street, Suite 349
New York, NY 10003

© 2011 The Brown Reference Group Ltd.

For Gareth Stevens Publishing:
Art Direction: Haley Harasymiw
Editorial Direction: Kerri O'Donnell

For The Brown Reference Group Ltd:
Editorial Director: Lindsey Lowe
Managing Editor: Tim Harris
Editor: Tom Jackson
Children's Publisher: Anne O'Daly
Design Manager: David Poole
Designer: Supriya Sahai
Picture Manager: Sophie Mortimer
Production Director: Alastair Gourlay

Picture Credits:
Front Cover: Brown Reference Group.

Inside: Corbis: DK Limited 7c, Louis Psihoyos 9br, 19c; iStockphoto: Bob Ainsworth 13t, Jim Jurica 29cl; Photolibrary: DeA Picture Library 18/19, 20; Science Photo Library: Jamie Chirinos 9t, Christian Darkin 21cr, Roger Harris 10; Shutterstock: 5br, Linda Bucklin 31, Catmando 14b. Terry David 23cr, Four Oaks 5cl Jean-Michel Girard 7t, Chris Harvey 4, Ralf Juergen Kraft 26, Christian   Markin 28, Andreas Mayer 23l, Paul B. Moore 25t, Peter Polak 3, Vaclav Volrab 17.

All Artworks The Brown Reference Group Ltd.

Printed in the United States of America
1 2 3 4 5 6 7 8 9 12 11 10

CPSIA compliance information: Batch #CS10GS: For further information contact Gareth Stevens, New York, New York at 1-800-542-2595.

CONTENTS

Any words that appear in the text in **bold** are explained in the glossary.

WHAT IS A DINOSAUR?

Many years ago, long before the first human being was born, Earth was ruled by giant **reptiles** called **dinosaurs**. They were the biggest and meanest animals to ever live—and die—on our planet.

Although they were taller than trees, as strong as a tank, and fierce enough to eat a person whole, the dinosaurs are all gone now. The last ones died out 65 million years ago, when a space rock the size of a mountain crashed into Earth. This massive bang rocked life on Earth, making dinosaurs—and a lot of other animals—**extinct**. Among the survivors were snakes, lizards, birds, and little hairy creatures called **mammals**. Eventually the mammals took over Earth, **evolving** into elephants, whales, lions, and you!

The dinosaurs were forgotten until about 200 years ago. When early people dug up giant dinosaur **skulls** and bones, they thought they were the remains of dragons or other made-up monsters. We now know there were hundreds of different types of dinosaurs. Many were much larger than animals are today, and it is hard to imagine what the world would have been like with giant creatures thundering across the land.

Stone Bones

All that is left of the dinosaurs are **fossils**. These are mainly hard bones, claws, and teeth that have turned to stone over millions of years.

UP CLOSE

A lot of what we know about dinosaurs comes from their mouths. Their teeth and bony beaks tell us what kinds of foods they ate.

BARYONYX

Armed with powerful claws and a long snout packed with teeth, *Baryonyx* was a water hunter. Like grizzly bears do today, it raided shallow pools for fish.

Baryonyx lived about 120 millions years ago. It walked on its hind legs and used its long, stiff tail to balance. Its powerful arms could have held its weight, but walking on all fours would have been difficult because both of the hands were armed with razor-sharp claws. The middle claw was a gigantic 12-inch (30-cm) hook. It would have been used to catch fish, as well as to rip apart food. And it was a very dangerous weapon in fights!

Long snout

Walking leg

Long claw

Fresh Meat

The fossils of *Baryonyx* have been found alongside large plant-eating dinosaurs. Scientists think that *Baryonyx* may have eaten the flesh of dead animals by poking its long snout inside their bodies.

UP CLOSE

Baryonyx used its long claws as fishing hooks. It waded through water and speared a fish with a claw, scooping it into its long mouth. The mouth was a bit like a crocodile's— and was good for snapping up slippery fish.

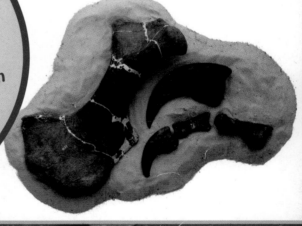

Name: *Baryonyx*
Pronounced: behr-ee-AH-nihks
Meaning of name: Heavy claw
Size: Up to 33 feet (10 m) long
Key features: Walked on hind legs; huge claw on front feet; long tail used for balance; crest on snout
Diet: Fish

CARCHARODON

There are only a few African dinosaurs we know about, and *Carcharodontosaurus* was one of the fiercest. Its 5-foot (1.5-m) skull was filled with immense teeth.

Few animals were safe from *Carcharodontosaurus*. It lived about 110 million years ago and preyed on plant-eating dinosaurs that were often even bigger than itself. The fierce dinosaur could run short distances on its large hind legs. It probably made surprise attacks by bursting out from a hiding place and knocking its victims to the ground.

...TOSAURUS

Lost Fossils

Very few *Carcharodontosaurus* fossils have been found. The best remains were found in 1925 in Egypt, but these bones were blown up during World War II.

Huge head

Small arms

Long tail

Bites and Kicks

Carcharodontosaurus is named for its teeth, which have a triangle shape like those of today's big sharks. The teeth were great at slicing into flesh, but the dinosaur probably stopped prey by kicking it to the ground before biting.

Name: Carcharodontosaurus
Pronounced: kahr-kahr-uh-dahn-tuh-SOHR-uhs
Meaning of name: Shark-toothed lizard
Size: Up to 43 feet (13 m) long
Key features: Two legs; large teeth
Diet: Large plant-eating dinosaurs

COMPSOGNA

We normally think dinosaurs were all lumbering giants, but *Compsognathus* was a fast-moving critter that ran around snapping up insects and lizards.

Compsognathus's body was small and slender. Most of its length was made up of a whiplike tail and a long, **flexible** neck. This dinosaur was always on the move, running after prey that scuttled and fluttered through its swampy home. All giant dinosaurs had to make turns carefully to avoid falling over. *Compsognathus* did not have this problem. Its flexible body allowed it to change direction very quickly. It could streak in zigzags across the ground when it chased prey. *Compsognathus* lived in the same area as the first birds. It may have been one of the world's first bird-eating animals.

Large eye

Long neck

Birdlike feet

UP CLOSE

Some scientists think that *Compsognathus* was covered in tufts that were a little like feathers.

THUS

Name: Compsognathus

Pronounced:
kahmp-sahg-NAY-thus

Meaning of name: Pretty jaw

Size: 4.5 feet (1.4 m) long

Key features: Flexible neck; long tail; fast runner; good eyesight

Diet: Small animals

Small Killer

Compsognathus was one of the smaller dinosaurs we know about. It was not much bigger than a turkey. It lived in the swampy woodlands of what is now northern Europe about 155 million years ago.

Two Fossils in One

One Compsognathus fossil has a lizard skeleton preserved inside of it. The dinosaur must have died right after it had finished a meal.

11

DEINONYCHUS

They were not the largest or strongest dinosaurs ever to live, but a gang of *Deinonychus* was one of the most dangerous things around in North America about 113 million years ago.

Dinosaurs are not known for being clever. Most had very small brains compared to the size of their bodies. However, *Deinonychus* was one of the brainy ones. Experts think this dinosaur's skin was **camouflaged** with stripes and blotches, and a *Deinonychus* hid in the undergrowth waiting for the right time to strike. Once it had planned an attack, few prey got away. The hunter could slice open a victim's belly with one slash of its monstrous claw.

Long snout

Name: *Deinonychus*
Pronounced: dy-NAH-nih-kuhs
Meaning of name: Terrible claw
Size: 10 feet (3 m) long
Key features: Heavy claw on middle toe; lived in **packs**; probably striped for camouflage
Diet: Large plant eaters

Pack Attack

Deinonychus probably hunted in packs—like wolves do today. The hunters worked together to kill large prey, taking it in turns to slash the animal until it collapsed, **exhausted**.

UP CLOSE

Deinonychus also weakened its prey with savage bites. Its teeth had sawlike edges that sliced flesh into chunks. Its snout was narrow, so it could squeeze through wounds into the middle of dead bodies to get at tasty treats.

Long tail

Hooked claw

Hooked

Deinonychus's hooked claw was on a flexible toe. It was raised up off the ground so it did not become blunted by stones. During an attack, the claw could slash through a half circle, ripping into the victim.

DIPLODOCUS

Nothing much about this dinosaur was small. An adult *Diplodocus* was longer than a tennis court, thanks to a huge tail and a long neck. It weighed three times as much as an African elephant!

Like giraffes do today, *Diplodocus* used its neck to reach higher than other plant eaters to get at the very freshest leaves at the tops of tall trees. Its mouth was filled with peglike teeth. The teeth worked like a rake, tugging the leaves from their stalks. *Diplodocus* had very thick legs to hold its weight. The neck and tail bones were **hollow** to make them lighter. The head was the size of a modern horse's—any larger and the dinosaur would not have been strong enough to lift it up.

Long neck

Small head

Thick leg

14

Stomach Stones

As well as munching on fresh leaves from the treetops, *Diplodocus* also swallowed stones! This was because the giant did not have enough teeth to chew its food. Instead it swallowed the leaves whole, and they were ground up in the stomach by the stones.

Herd Life

Diplodocus probably lived in herds, like elephants and giraffes do today. The baby dinosaurs would have stayed in the middle of the group. If any hunting dinosaur tried to attack, an adult on the edge of the herd would give them a whack with its enormous tail– or a hefty kick!

Name: *Diplodocus*

Pronounced: dy-PLAH-duh-kuhs

Meaning of name: Double beam

Size: Up to 88 feet (27 m) long

Key features: Small head; sturdy body; long neck and tail

Diet: Leaves and ferns

GIGANOTOSA

f this dinosaur were not real, we would have to make it up. It could fit into any monster movie. It was large enough to look over the top of a house and could snap you up in a single, enormous bite.

Dinosaurs are known for being big. Some of the plant-eating dinosaurs were the largest animals to ever walk on Earth. But even these giants had an enemy—*Giganotosaurus*. This huge killer hunted in fast-running packs, tearing chunks out of victims with their long teeth. Nothing was safe.

Clawed hands

Sturdy legs

Tail for balance

URUS

Name: *Giganotosaurus*
Pronounced:
jy-guh-nah-toh-SOHR-uhs
Meaning of name: Giant southern lizard
Size: 43 feet (13 m) long
Key features: Two legs; big jaw
Diet: Big plant eaters

UP CLOSE

Giganotosaurus was one of the largest dinosaur hunters ever. Its teeth were longer than a person's hand, and a 10-year-old child could lie down in its mouth—although it would not have been very comfortable!

Monster Find

The first *Giganotosaurus* fossil was found in 1995, buried in rocks in South America. Scientists were amazed to find a dinosaur that was larger, stronger, and even more deadly than a *Tyrannosaurus rex*.

17

MEGALOSAURUS

This fierce hunter stalked its prey across Europe about 180 million years ago. It was the first animal ever to be named a dinosaur—and started the search for many more long-dead monsters.

Scientists have found *Megalosaurus* bones and footprints preserved in rocks. The footprints tell us how this giant hunter would have walked. It turns out that *Megalosaurus* was pigeon-toed—it walked with its hind feet turned toward each other. But that did not stop it from running at high speed during hunts. It charged forward with its tail raised up for balance and snatched prey with its clawed hands.

Strong tail

Free Meals

Some *Megalosaurus* fossils have been found on beaches. Scientists think these shoreline dinosaurs did not always hunt for food. They also survived by eating the bodies of large, oceangoing reptiles that had washed up on the beach.

Name: *Megalosaurus*
Pronounced: meh-guh-loh-SOHR-uhs
Meaning of name: Great lizard
Size: 26 feet (8 m) long
Key features: Walked on two legs; large claws on hands and feet; large head with sharp teeth
Diet: Small dinosaurs and **marine** reptiles

Saw-like teeth

Small arms

UP CLOSE

Megalosaurus had teeth with jagged edges like a steak knife. They were also hooked, making it harder for prey to struggle free.

FEATURE

Megalosaurus fossils were the first dinosaur remains to be studied by scientists. In 1824, English experts showed that the bones belonged to giant reptiles that they named dinosaurs, meaning "terrible lizards."

OVIRAPTOR

Did you think that all dinosaurs had huge, pointed teeth? Well, this one didn't have a single tooth. It had a horny beak a bit a like parrot's, only ten times bigger! Even without teeth, *Oviraptor* could give a bite to remember.

Oviraptor lived in Asia about 80 million years ago. Its long back legs and shortish tail tell us that it could run fast when it needed to. However, we do not know much about what it ate. One fossil has been found with a lizard skeleton in its stomach, so maybe *Oviraptor* chased its victims and grabbed them with its free hands. However, the dinosaur's beak is better suited to crack hard shells, so *Oviraptor* may have also collected large seeds or shellfish.

Headgear

It is possible that *Oviraptor*s had crests on their heads. These might have been very colorful and used by the males to show off to the females. A bird called the cassowary uses a similar crest in the same way.

Beak

20

Run, Dino, Run!

Oviraptor was built for running. It had to move fast to stay out of the way of the much bigger hunters that were always on the lookout for a snack. The closest thing we have to an *Oviraptor* today is the ostrich.

Small head

Claws on hands

Flexible feet

Name: *Oviraptor*
Pronounced: OH-vuh-rap-tohr
Meaning of name: Egg thief
Size: 8 feet (2.5 m) long
Key features: Long hind leg; flexible arms
Diet: Seeds, shellfish

UP CLOSE

Several *Oviraptor* fossils were found near eggs, so people thought that the dinosaur stole eggs to eat. However, experts now know that the eggs had baby *Oviraptors* inside—they were not food but a dinosaur nest!

SPINOSAURUS

It is one of the biggest hunters in history, but was *Spinosaurus* all that fierce? It was a monster, but experts think that *Spinosaurus* just liked to pick on small animals.

Imagine an animal that is as long as a train car with a head like a crocodile and teeth and claws as long as your fingers. Then add a scaly fin rising out of its back! This is *Spinosaurus*. It lived in Africa about 95 million years ago. Scientists think that *Spinosaurus* walked on its back legs and probably hunted in shallow water. It snapped up fish with its toothy snout. With a head as big as a bathtub, it could take quite a mouthful.

Big Sail

No one knows what *Spinosaurus* used its fin for. It could have been a way of showing off to mates and **rivals**, or it might have been a heating system that picked up the warmth of the sun on cold days. Whatever it was for, the sail was **fragile**, so *Spinosaurus* stayed out of fights.

Sail-shaped fin

Tooth

UP CLOSE

Spinosaurus had pointed teeth in a long jaw a bit like a crocodile's. Experts think this head shape shows that Spinosaurus hunted in water.

Claw

Name: Spinosaurus
Pronounced: spy-nuh-SOHR-uhs
Meaning of name: Spine lizard
Size: 39 feet (12 m) long
Key features: Large spiny sail on the back; long head packed with teeth
Diet: Fish and other water animals

TRICERATOPS

It is no surprise that this big beast is one of the most familiar of all dinosaurs—you would not forget those giant horns in a hurry. Despite its tough look, *Triceratops* was a peaceful plant eater—unless it was under attack!

Triceratops was the dinosaur version of a rhino. It lived in North America about 70 million years ago and survived by munching on tough leaves and twigs. It evolved its fearsome horns as defense against something just as frightening—*Tyrannosaurus rex*! *T. rex* liked to kill with a bite to the neck, but *Triceratops* had a frill of bone shielding this weak point. *Triceratops* was almost attack proof!

Neck shield

Horn

Big Heads

Triceratops had several relatives, all with horns poking out of their faces. They also had massive heads. *Triceratops*'s head was 6.5 feet (2 m) long, but its cousin *Pentaceratops* (it had five horns) had a head 9.75 feet (3 m) long. This was the largest head of any land animal—ever!

Bendy Face

Most dinosaurs could not chew their food, but *Triceratops* had flexible cheeks. They allowed its toothless beak to bend from side to side—slicing up the woody food.

Name: *Triceratops*
Pronounced: try-SEHR-uh-tahps
Meaning of name:
Three-horned face
Size: 30 feet (9 m) long
Key features: Large head with three horns; bony shield over neck
Diet: Twigs and leaves

Beak

TYRANNOS

Seventy million years ago, *Tyrannosaurus* ruled North America. Its full name is *Tyrannosaurus rex*, which means "King of the Tyrant Lizards." With the biggest bite around, nothing could win against a *T. rex!*

Scientists think *Tyrannosaurus* had one of the most powerful bites in history. Its jaws could crush bodies, bones and all. No one knows how *Tyrannosaurus* caught prey. Its arms were too short to reach its mouth, so its only weapon was its mighty mouth. It probably crept up on victims, and then attacked with a high-speed charge.

UP CLOSE

A *Tyrannosaurus* tooth was the size and shape of a banana—but a lot sharper. This dinosaur killed prey with a bite to the neck, the same way a lion kills today.

AURUS

Name: *Tyrannosaurus rex*
Pronounced: ty-raa-nuh-SOHR-uhs
Meaning of name: Tyrant lizard
Size: 49 feet (15 m) long
Key features: Big head with powerful bite; walked on back legs; very small arms with two fingers
Diet: Smaller dinosaurs

Large nostril

Eye

Smeller

Tyrannosaurus had a great sense of smell. Some scientists think it was too slow to catch living prey, so it sniffed out dead animals to eat.

Hooked teeth

Birdlike Beast

Scientists think birds evolved from small cousins of *Tyrannosaurus*. They all have similar skeletons. Some suggest that *Tyrannosaurus* also had feathers all over its body.

VELOCIRAPTOR

Few dinosaurs are movie stars. *Velociraptor* became famous after appearing in the *Jurassic Park* movies, where it terrified audiences with its deadly killing tactics.

Velociraptor lived in Asia about 80 million years ago. It was a small dinosaur, but was still an expert killer. Scientists have suggested that *Velociraptors* hunted in teams, like lions do today. Some of them drove prey out into the open, where the rest of the pack was waiting. The *Velociraptors* worked together to kill victims that were too large for one *Velociraptor* on its own.

High Speed

Velociraptors were very fast runners. Their long hind legs could carry them at speeds of 37 miles (60 km) per hour—twice as fast as a person can move. To stay balanced at top speeds, they held out their stiff tails behind them.

Smart Killer

Experts believe that *Velociraptor* was a clever and **cunning** hunter. It probably followed its chosen prey over long distances. It had large, forward-facing eyes, so it could keep track of its victim during a high-speed chase.

Large eye

UP CLOSE

Velociraptor was well armed. It probably killed its prey by holding it down with its clawed hands and slashing with one foot. The longest toe claws could slice open the victim's belly.

Name: *Velociraptor*
Pronounced: vuh-LAH-suh-rap-tohr
Meaning of name: Fast thief
Size: 6.5 feet (2 m) long
Key features: Long snout; sharp teeth; hooked claws on hands and feet
Diet: Small, plant-eating dinosaurs

Claw

Long leg

GLOSSARY

camouflaged Colored so that the body blends in with the surroundings, making it easier for an animal to hide.

cunning Able to plan ahead and trick other animals.

dinosaur A type of reptile that lived between 230 and 65 million years ago.

evolved When a living thing has changed very slowly over many years to adapt to changes in the environment.

exhausted So tired that the body cannot move anymore.

extinct When every member of a species (type of animal or other living thing) has died out.

flexible Bendy, not stiff.

fossil The remains of a dead animal or other living thing that have been preserved in rock. Most fossils are of hard body parts, such as bones.

fragile Easily broken or harmed.

hollow To have no solid center.

mammal An animal that has hairs on at least some of its body and feeds its young with its own milk.

marine Coming from or belonging to the ocean.

pack A group of animals—usually hunters—which work together to find enough food to survive.

prey An animal that is hunted by another animal.

reptile An animal with scaly skin. A reptile is cold-blooded, which means that its temperature varies with its surroundings. Dinosaurs were reptiles. Modern reptiles include snakes, turtles, and lizards.

rivals Others that want the same thing as you and need to be defeated.

skeleton All the bones in a body, which join together to give it its shape.

skull The bones making up an animal's head.

snout An animal's nose and jaws.

Books about dinosaurs

Dalla Vecchia, Fabio Marco. *Giganotosaurus.* Detroit, MI: Blackbirch Press, 2007.

Malam, John. *Dinosaur Atlas.* New York, NY: Dorling Kindersley, 2006.

Mash, Robert. *Extreme Dinosaurs.* New York, NY: Atheneum, 2007.

Matthews, Rupert. *Dinosaur Combat: Unearth the Secrets Behind Dinosaur Fossils.* Laguna Hills, CA: QEB Publishing, 2008.

Useful Web sites

Dinosaurs for Kids
http://www.kidsdinos.com/

National Geographic Kids: Dinosaurs
http://kids.nationalgeographic.com/Games/PuzzlesQuizzes/Brainteaserdinosaurs

PBS Kids: Dinosaur Train
http://pbskids.org/dinosaurtrain/

INDEX